Constructions for Children
Projects in Design Technology

◆

Barbara Eichelberger
and
Connie Larson

Dale Seymour Publications

Acknowledgments

We express our appreciation to the Gladstone School District for providing an environment that encourages creativity and growth.

A loving thank-you to our children, who shared their enthusiasm, their eagerness to learn, and their faith in us.

Managing Editor: Michael Kane
Project Editor: Joan Gideon
Production Coordinator: Barbara Atmore
Cover Design: Rachel Gage
Illustrations: Susan Cronin-Paris

Order Number DS21200
ISBN 0-86651-627-1
3 4 5 6 7 8 9 10–MA–96 95 94

DALE
SEYMOUR
PUBLICATIONS
P.O. BOX 10888
PALO ALTO, CA 94303

This book is printed on recycled paper.

Contents

Introduction

Children learn best when they are actively participating in the learning process. The educational approach called *Design Technology* serves that premise well. *Design Technology* is a blend of science and invention; it allows children to be involved in problem solving in the real world. It gives them the capability and the confidence to design, construct, and evaluate working models. If you are not familiar with the approach, this collection of hands-on, child-centered activities will serve as an introduction. The list of professional resources at the end of this book offers further reading on the subject, as well as other ideas for creative and open-ended construction projects.

The projects in this book are suitable for inventors of any age and are especially enjoyed by students in grades K–4. Many make ideal cooperative activities. In completing these projects, there is never one right way or one right answer. That is *Design Technology's* joy and its challenge. The amount of assistance you need in pulling the projects together will depend on your previous experiences—and the same holds for your students. Some will need more guidance and assistance than others, but as each student's knowledge and confidence increases, the need for assistance decreases.

This guide contains a detailed, step-by-step explanation for each project to get you started on a particular type of model. Photographs and line drawings are included to help you picture the possibilities each project holds. However, please do not think of these instructions as prescriptive— they are guidelines only. We know that as you gain experience with this exciting educational approach, you will begin to problem solve and create new challenges of your own.

Of particular use to beginners will be the section of each project called "Snags and Suggestions." While we can't possibly predict every situation that may develop in your classroom or give you answers for each and every question or concern your students will raise, we have shared some common project flaws, as well as some possible questions your students may want to explore further.

Materials

The materials list for each project alerts you to the types of items and tools you will need for an entire class. Some projects call for empty boxes, plastic food containers, or lids—things you might want to be collecting all year, with help from your students and their families. Many of the items are standard school supplies. Others will require a special order or special purchase for particular projects. Some may be a little tricky to find, depending on your location. For example, syringes and vinyl tubing are sometimes called for; to find these, check scientific supply companies or local variety stores and drugstores. In the beginning, you may find yourself a visitor to building and hardware stores, craft and fabric stores, toy and hobby shops, and scientific supply centers, scouting out interesting materials that will enhance the projects. You may also develop a network of contacts at local businesses, warehouses, and factories—places that can help you locate certain specialty items.

Always be aware of safety when handling materials and tools. Within each project, we have indicated when an adult needs to help students use a saw, an awl, or a hot-glue gun. For the projects that use syringes, use oral medication syringes, which have no needles, or remove and safely dispose of the needles before you bring syringes to the classroom. Children need to understand that a used hypodermic syringe can be very dangerous. Caution them that if they should ever find a syringe, they should not touch it.

Presenting a Theme-Based Integrated Project

One of the strengths of these projects is the way they lend themselves to a theme-based, integrated curriculum. Starting with a theme, such as Space or Marsupials, you can choose a variety of *Design Technology* projects that relate to the theme, and then plan ways to integrate activities in math, literature, writing, oral language, art, drama and movement, and social and current events.

We always introduce a new theme through a quality children's literature book. A short list of related literature is included with each project to give you some ideas of where you might start. For example, read Maurice Sendak's *Where the Wild Things Are,* and then have students construct Max's boat; or present *Angela's Airplane* by Robert Munsch, and then build an airplane.

After we have hooked the students into wanting to do more with a topic, we talk about possible *Design Technology* projects that could be related to the theme. Once students have become familiar with the various design systems involved in these projects (such as pneumatic power or gears, listed on page ix), we sometimes suggest that they think about ways to develop a particular design system, especially one that we haven't worked with for a while. But many times, students will come up with great ideas for projects on their own.

Suppose we were to start by reading *The Magic Fan* by Keith Baker. We would then ask students if they knew what type of bridge Yoshi had constructed. Then we would hold a brainstorming session to find out what students knew about bridges in general. We would list this information on a chart or web and then give everyone time to gather additional information about bridges from any source. During this information gathering, students could be working with partners or in small cooperative groups. After students had shared in class their newly acquired information about bridges, we would present the inventing challenge. Here's one such challenge:

◆ Create a bridge that allows a vehicle 6 inches wide to cross it.

Once the purpose of the project is clearly established, the first step for students is to think on paper. This is the invention step; we also call it pre-design. It not only allows thinking time, it also aids in the conservation of materials. The next step would be the actual construction. During construction, students often find that some modifications of their pre-design may be necessary. This is real problem solving in action!

When the projects are finished, students write about their work. This technical writing reflects how they made their bridges, the problems they encountered and solved, and their feelings of accomplishment. They make and label technical drawings of the bridges to accompany their writing, doing the drawings to scale whenever they are developmentally ready to do so. Even the youngest students complete this phase of the project, freely using invented spelling as needed. After students have completed their technical writings and drawings, we lead them into a variety of theme-related work in other curriculum areas.

Design Systems

The inventions in our collection are based on nine different design systems. Each is used independently in making these particular models, but they could be combined into many more-complex projects, especially with older students. Following are the design systems that we encourage our students to become familiar with:

Gravity power: A force that creates acceleration in a downward motion. This force can be encouraged in many ways. Experimentation with different lengths, as of ramps, or with different angles, as of the slant of a wire, can become a part of the challenge.

Rubber-band power: The use of twisted or wrapped rubber bands for storing energy. Experimentation can be done to determine what size of rubber band is best for storing the most energy.

Pneumatic power: The use of air as an energy source. Balloons, syringes, hair dryers, fans, and natural wind are the sources used most often. Experimentation may focus on the positioning of the air source.

Hydraulic power: The use of water or different densities of oil for the power source. Syringes and tubing are used. A sampling of syringes and tubing of different sizes, holding different liquids, is a good model for students to view.

Gears: The use of cogged wheels to transfer motion from one wheel to another. Gears can be made with heavy paper, wooden matches, toothpicks, skewers, chopsticks, tongue depressors, ice cream sticks, or doweling. Corrugated paper reinforced with toothpicks makes a very sturdy gear also.

Lever: A projecting piece that transmits and modifies force or motion when another force is applied. This force can be a pulling force, as with the use of string, or a force that works around pivot points. Figuring out the pivot points is the challenge.

Crank: The movement of a bent shaft to create circular motion. Shafts with a right angle can be bent from wire. Experimentation with the appropriate number of right angles and the best placement of them is the challenge.

Marionette: A figure with jointed limbs that is moved from above by manipulation of threads, yarns, strings, fishing lines, or wires. With small children, yarn or string is easier to handle.

Structure: Something built in a definite pattern of organization. Rolled paper makes a very sturdy structure. Straws, pipe cleaners, and triangular paper corners can also be used.

Junk Construction

Junk construction is an important component of *Design Technology*. For this type of project, you will need to keep a classroom construction center well supplied with recycled materials of every shape and kind. During junk construction there is little teacher assistance and whatever the children construct is accepted. Junk construction has two purposes: one is to give children an opportunity to create their own challenges and to construct freely; the other is for children to explore freely a given design system. Junk construction also provides a time for you to observe and guide children in the safe handling of tools and materials.

The rest of this book is devoted to twenty stimulating projects we have used successfully with our students. Remember that each project is open-ended. We hope you will use them to bring another dimension to your curriculum. Happy constructing!

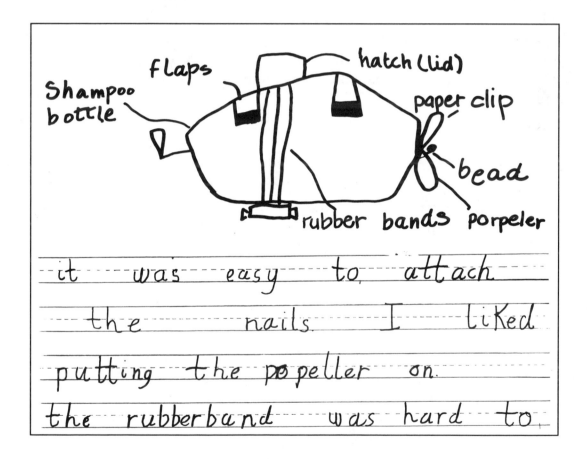

it was easy to attach
the nails. I liked
putting the popeller on.
the rubberband was hard to

Gravity-Powered Vehicle

Sturdy boxes ◆ Craft supplies for decoration
Doweling ◆ Saw ◆ Heavy rubber bands
Wheels (spools, ribbon reels, lids, film canisters, wooden wheels)
Spacers (small pieces of vinyl tubing, beads, cork, straws)
Masking tape ◆ Board for a ramp

Construction

Note: Adult help will be needed when cutting the doweling in step 2.

1. Wrap, paint, or decorate a sturdy box.
2. Cut the doweling for the axles. The pieces need to be the width of the box plus the width of four spacers and two wheels. Add just a little extra space. Don't forget to make two axles.
3. Connect as many heavy rubber bands as is necessary to attach the doweling to the box, going over the top of the box.
4. Mount each of the wheels on the doweling by putting a spacer next to the box, then a wheel, and then a spacer. If necessary, secure the last spacer with tape.

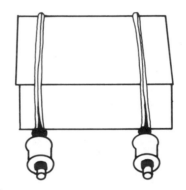

5. Add decorations to the vehicle that are appropriate for the theme.
6. Erect a ramp using a board of other sturdy material and use it to give the vehicle its gravity power.

Snags and Suggestions

◆ If your vehicle does not roll down the ramp straight, check the axles. Are they crooked? How could you make the vehicle go straight?

◆ Why does your vehicle go farther than someone else's?
Do some vehicles go faster than others?

◆ Are your wheels turning freely? Check for friction. How could you eliminate friction?

◆ Measure the distance the vehicles travel. Try using different heights for the ramp. Make a graph to compare the distance traveled by the different vehicles. Or make a graph to compare the height of the ramp to the distance traveled for a specific vehicle.

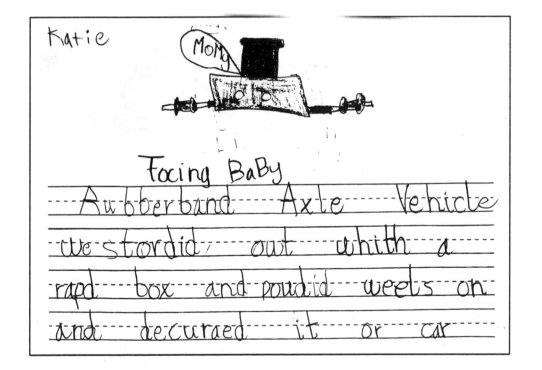

Katie

MoM

Facing BaBy

Rubberband Axle Vehicle

we stordid out whith a

rapd box and poudid weels on

and decuraed it or car

Related Literature

Fowler, Richard. *Mr. Little's Noisy Car.* New York: Putnam, 1987.
Williams, Karen Lynn. *Galimoto.* New York: Mulberry Books, 1990.

Gravity-Powered, Inserted-Axle Vehicle

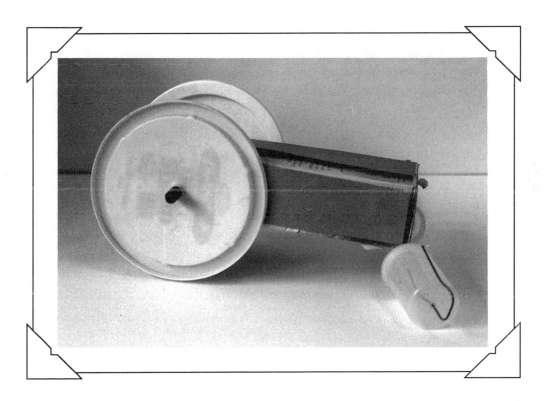

Materials

Sturdy boxes • Craft supplies for decoration
Wire or doweling • Saw • Wire cutters • Awl
Wheels (spools, ribbon reels, lids, film canisters, wooden wheels)
Masking tape or hot-glue gun
Spacers (small pieces of vinyl tubing, beads, cork, straws)
Board for a ramp

Construction

Note: Adult help will be needed when cutting the axles in step 4, when using the awl in step 5 and step 6, and when using the hot-glue gun in step 6.

1. Wrap a box in colored paper or paint it.
2. Select a material for the axles. Wire makes a good axle for film canister wheels; doweling works well for lids or wooden wheels.
3. Choose spacers appropriate for the wheels and axles.
4. Cut the axles. Make sure the length of each axle will accommodate the box, two wheels, and four spacers with a little extra space.
5. Decide where the holes for the axles will go. Use an awl to punch the holes. Be sure to keep the axles perpendicular to the sides of the box. Insert each axle through the box.
6. Punch holes in the wheels and assemble a spacer, the wheel, and the other spacer on the axle on each side of the box. The last spacer may need to be secured with masking tape or with hot glue.

7. Decorate the vehicle to correspond to the theme.

8. Erect a ramp using a board of other sturdy material and use it to give the vehicle its gravity power.

Snags and Suggestions

◆ This is an excellent place to use measurement to ensure that your axles are placed correctly. Before you make holes for the axles, measure the same distance up from the bottom of the box on both sides and the same distance in from the front or back. What happens to your vehicle's movement if the axles are not placed correctly?

◆ With junk-box vehicles, the choice of materials is endless and inexpensive. Not only can you decorate the box, but you can add to it. Let your imagination soar!

- ◆ Be careful in your planning. Wheels need to touch the ground.
- ◆ If the wheels are on the ground and do not turn, check for friction. How could you eliminate friction?
- ◆ Measure the distance the vehicles travel. Try using different heights for the ramp. Make a graph to compare the distance traveled by the different vehicles. Or make a graph to compare the height of the ramp to the distance traveled for a specific vehicle.

Related Literature

Biro, Val. *Gumdrop* (series). Milwaukee, Wis.: Gareth Stevens, 1986.

Crews, Donald. *Trucks*. New York: Franklin Watts, 1982.

Rubber Band–Powered, Inserted-Axle Vehicle

Materials

Sturdy boxes ◆ Craft supplies for decorating ◆ Doweling
Wheels (spools, ribbon reels, lids, wooden wheels)
Awl ◆ Saw ◆ Spacers (vinyl tubing, straws, beads)
Hot-glue gun ◆ Heavy rubber bands
Masking tape ◆ Large paper clips

Construction

Note: Adult help will be needed when cutting the doweling in step 2, when using the awl in step 3, and when using the hot-glue gun in step 5.

1. Select a sturdy box. The top of the box must be open. Wrap the box in colored paper if desired.
2. Make your wheel and spacer selections. Then cut the doweling a little longer than the width of the box plus two wheels and two spacers.
3. The open side of the box will be the bottom of the vehicle. Use the awl to make holes for the axles, making sure the wheels will touch the ground. Insert the axles through the box.
4. Assemble a spacer and a wheel on each side of each axle.
5. Secure the wheel to the axle with a hot-glue gun. It is essential that the wheel and axle move as one. In the gravity-powered vehicles, the wheels turn and the axle remains stable. In the rubber band–powered vehicle, the axle turns with the wheel.

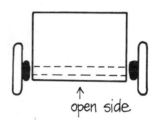

6. Connect two or more sturdy rubber bands.
7. Attach the end of one of the rubber bands to the center of one axle with masking tape. This axle becomes the rear axle.
8. Punch a hole in the end of the box opposite the rear axle.
9. Attach a large paper clip to end of the other rubber band. Going under the front axle, thread the rubber band through the opening in the box. Turn the paper clip to secure the rubber band.

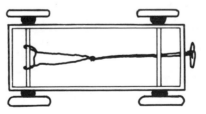

10. Decorate the vehicle according to your chosen theme.
11. The construction of your vehicle is completed. Now you can experiment with the energy and direction. Wind up your vehicle by turning the back wheels.

Snags and Suggestions

◆ Energy from the rubber band may be released too quickly. You can add weight to the vehicle to alleviate spinout.
◆ Why does one vehicle go farther than another? Does placement of the weight make a difference? Does the number of times the wheels were wound up make a difference?
◆ If your vehicle isn't going straight, check your axles.
◆ If an axle is not turning freely, check for and eliminate friction.
◆ Measure the distance each vehicle travels. Make a graph comparing the distance your vehicle travels to the number of times the back wheels were turned to wind the rubber bands.

Related Literature

Gauch, Patricia Lee. *Christina Katerina and the Box*. New York: Putnam, 1980.

Pringle, Lawrence. *Jesse Builds a Road*. New York: Macmillan, 1987.

Rubber Band–
Powered Airplane

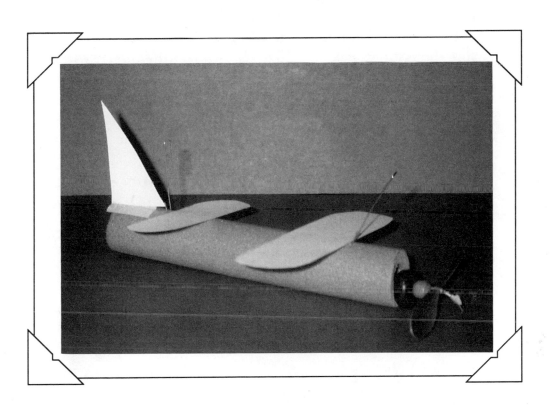

Materials

Heavy rubber bands • Small paper clips or wire
Thread spools • Washer material (tagboard, plastic)
Scissors • Awl or paper punch • Beads
Pipe insulation or paper towel roll
Propeller pattern on page 16
Heavy paper or lightweight cardboard
Craft materials for decorating • Large paper clips • Fishing line

Construction

Note: Adult help will be needed when using the awl in steps 4 and 9.

1. Connect together two rubber bands.
2. If you are using paper clips instead of wire, open and straighten a small paper clip, leaving the small hook on one end. Make sure the rest of the paper clip is very straight. If you use wire, make a hook in one end.
3. Attach the connected rubber bands to the hooked end of the paper clip or wire and close the hook.
4. Cut out a washer the size of the end of the spool and punch a hole in the center.
5. If you are making your own propeller, trace the pattern onto a plastic milk carton and cut it out.
6. Thread the spool, washer, bead, and propeller onto the straightened paper clip. Bend the paper clip over the propeller to secure.
7. Thread the rubber band through a 9-inch piece of pipe insulation or paper towel roll that forms the body of the airplane. Secure the rubber bands with a large paper clip.

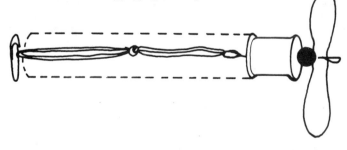

8. Design and cut from heavy paper a piece for the front wings, a smaller piece for the back wings, and a tail. You can experiment with different shapes, but keep them small and light-weight. Attach the wings and tail to the body of the plane.
9. Make two small holes in the front and in the back of the plane. Partially straighten two large paper clips and insert them through these holes as hooks.
10. Stretch the fishing line across the room. Attach it to opposite walls as a track for the airplanes.

11. Wind the propeller tightly and hold it.
12. Place the paper clip hooks over the fishing line and release the propeller.

Snags and Suggestions

◆ Have you discovered how straight your paper clip needs to be?

◆ If you are having trouble with your airplane not moving a great distance, focus on the number of times you wind the propeller. Does it make a difference if you wind it twenty-five times or fifty times?

◆ If you become frustrated, let gravity help. Lower one end of the fishing line.

◆ Measure the distance the plane travels. Make a graph that shows the distance traveled by each plane. Make a graph to compare the distance one plane travels with the number of times the propeller was wound.

Related Literature

McPhail, David. *First Flight*. Boston: Little, Brown, 1987.
Spier, Peter. *Bored—Nothing to Do!* New York: Doubleday, 1987.

Rubber Band–
Powered Submarine

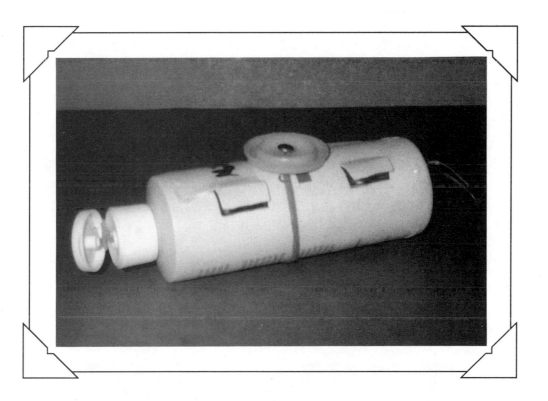

Materials

Shampoo bottles with flip-top lids • Sharp knife • Awl
Heavy rubber bands • Small paper clips • Beads
Propeller pattern on page 16
Hook made from a coat hanger • Large nails
Brads • Small lids • Water table or wading pool

Construction

Note: Adult help will be needed when using the sharp knife in step 1 and when using the awl in steps 2, 3, and 11.

1. Cut four 1-inch flaps in a shampoo bottle—two on each side.

2. Punch two holes in the bottle on what will be the bottom of the submarine—one in the front and one in the back.
3. Punch one hole in the center of the end of the bottle.
4. Connect as many rubber bands as needed for the length of the shampoo bottle.
5. Open and straighten a small paper clip, leaving a hook on one end. Attach the connected rubber bands to the hooked end of the paper clip, and close the hook.

6. Going through a flap nearest the bottom of the bottle, push the straight end of the paper clip through the end hole. Allow the rubber bands to hang loosely inside the bottle.

7. If you are making your own propeller, trace the pattern onto a plastic milk carton and cut it out.

8. Thread a bead and then a propeller onto the paper clip. Bend the paper clip over the propeller to secure it.

9. Use the hook made from a piece of coat hanger to catch the rubber band and pull it through the neck and lid of the bottle. Secure the end of the rubber band around the flip part of the bottle lid.

10. Put two rubber bands around the body of the bottle. Slip one or two large nails under these rubber bands at the bottom of the submarine. The nails add weight to the bottom of the submarine and, like a keel, keep the submarine balanced.

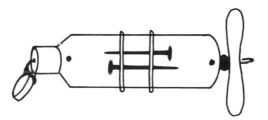

11. Punch a hole in any small lid that can represent a conning tower—the raised structure on the top deck. Make a hole on the top of the submarine and attach the conning tower with a brad.

12. Using the propeller, wind the rubber bands tightly. Submerge the completed submarine and release the propeller.

Snags and Suggestions

◆ If the propeller is wound tightly but is not turning, check for friction around the propeller.

◆ Why is the keel important to a boat or submarine? Leave the nails off your submarine and see what happens.

◆ What happens if you place one end of a piece of vinyl tubing inside the submerged submarine and blow?

◆ Replace worn out rubber bands after continued use.

Related Literature

Pallotta, Jerry. *The Underwater Alphabet Book*. Boston: Quinlan Press, 1991.

Tokuda, Wendy, and Richard Hall. *Humphrey, The Lost Whale*. Union City, Calif.: Heian International, 1989.

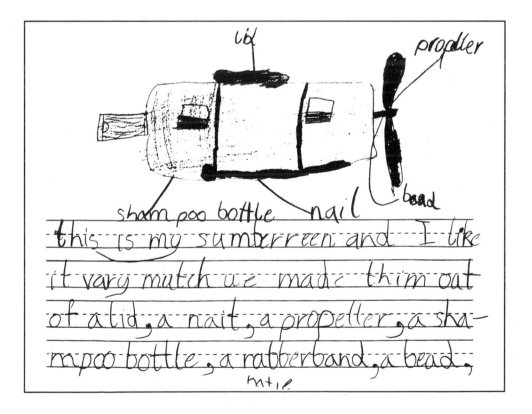

Rubber Band–
Powered Paddle Boat

Materials

Half-gallon and quart milk cartons
Scissors • Stapler
Garden stakes or doweling
Saw • Masking tape • Heavy rubber bands
Water table or wading pool

Construction

Note: Adult help will be needed when using the saw in step 2.

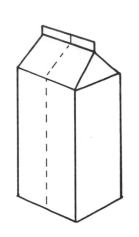

1. Cut a half-gallon milk carton in half lengthwise. Staple together the open end of the carton.
2. Cut garden stakes into 12-inch lengths.
3. With masking tape, attach two stakes to the two cut sides of the milk carton. Extend the stakes beyond the bottom end of the milk carton to accommodate the paddle.
4. Cut a quart milk carton into four equal sections. Cut these sections in half along the edge of the carton. You will have enough pieces for two paddle boats. Staple four sections together to form the paddle.

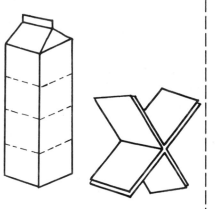

5. Loop a rubber band around the extended stakes, insert the paddle, and wind it.

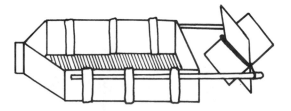

6. Holding the wound paddle, place the boat in water that is at least 3 inches deep.

Snags and Suggestions

◆ If there is not enough movement, try a larger or smaller rubber band.

◆ If the stakes do not hold with masking tape, try a rubber band around the body of the boat.

◆ How would modifications change the speed or direction of the boat?

◆ Measure the time and distance the boats travel, and graph the results.

Related Literature

Allen, Pamela. *Who Sank the Boat?* New York: Putnam, 1985.
Gramatky, Hardie. *Little Toot.* New York: Putnam, 1959.

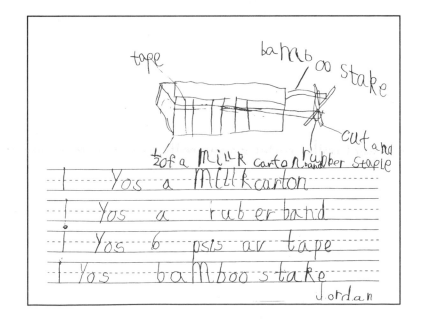

Rubber Band–Powered Rocket

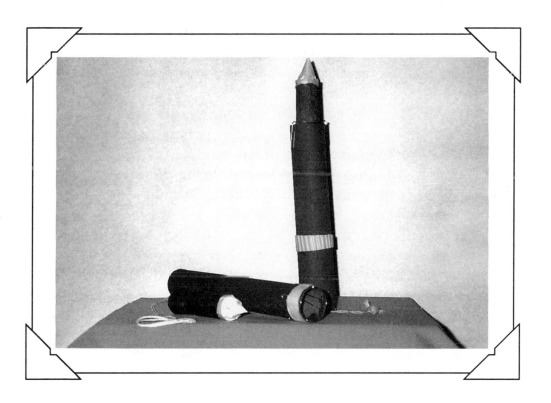

Materials

Cardboard tubing
(paper towel rolls, toilet paper rolls, wrapping paper rolls)
Scissors • Masking tape • Cardboard for cone
Large paper clips • Heavy rubber bands
Thread spools • Heavy string

Construction

1. Paint toilet paper roll and 12-inch lengths of paper towel tubing or wrapping paper tubing.

2. Cut a lengthwise section out of toilet paper roll to decrease the diameter of the roll. Tape the toilet paper roll back together. The reason for decreasing the size of the toilet paper roll is to make it fit loosely inside the paper towel tubing, which will be used for the launcher.

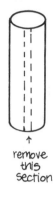

remove this section

3. Make a cone pattern by removing one quarter of a 3-inch-diameter circle. Trace the cone pattern on lightweight cardboard and cut it out.

4. Cut a length of masking tape and wrap it around one end of the toilet paper roll, leaving one half of the masking tape above the edge of the roll.

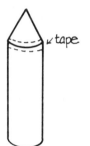

tape

5. Form the cone and insert it so that a little bit of the cone is inside the toilet paper roll. Press the tape onto the cone. Your rocket is now complete.

6. Attach two large paper clips to each of two sturdy rubber bands.

7. Use a spool that has several openings all the way through. Thread a 30-inch piece of heavy string through opposite openings. Where the string forms a loop on the end of the spool, insert the two rubber bands with the paper clips attached. Pull until tight. Knot the string at the opposite end of the spool.

loop

string

8. Drop the string through the paper towel tubing and attach the paper clips to the other end of the tubing. The launcher is now ready to fire the rocket.

9. Insert the rocket into the launcher. Pull back the string and release.

 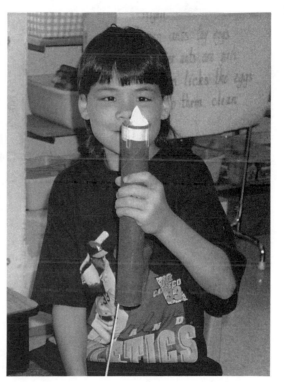

Snags and Suggestions

◆ If the paper clips come off your launcher, tape them down.

◆ Have you learned the importance of using sturdy rubber bands?

◆ If you would like to add a rocket booster, take a third piece of tubing and form it like the rocket. The sizes will need to be changed so the main rocket fits into the booster and the booster fits into the launcher.

◆ If you want to add a parachute to your rocket, muslin is a good choice of fabric.

◆ Measure the distance each rocket travels. You can make a graph to display the record distance for each rocket.

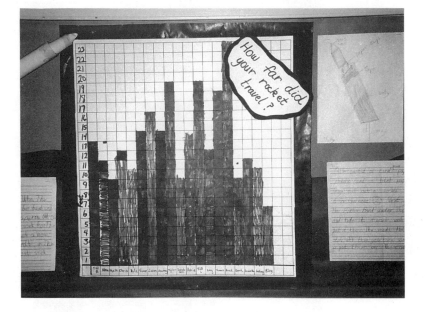

Related Literature

Eco, Umberto, and Eugenio Carmi. *The Three Astronauts.* San Diego, Calif.: Harcourt Brace Jovanovich, 1985.
Yorinks, Arthur. *Company's Coming.* New York: Crown, 1988.

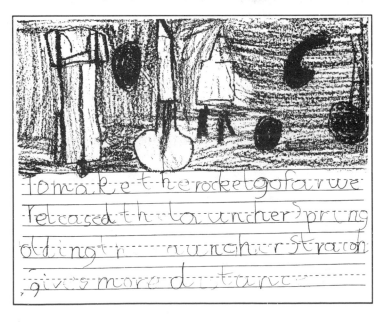

Pneumatic-Powered Airplane

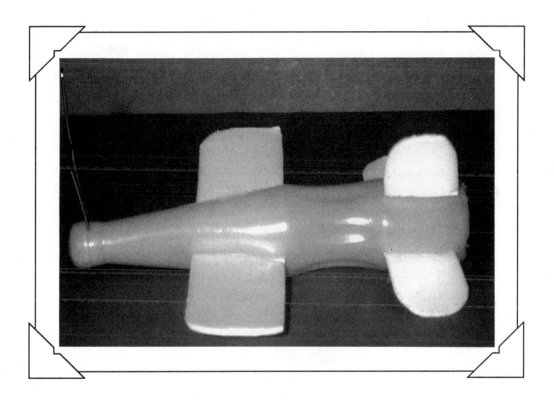

Materials

Wing and tail material
(plastic foam, cardboard, lightweight wood,
tongue depressors, ice cream sticks)
Squeezable juice drink bottles • Scissors • Awl
Large paper clips • Balloons
Masking tape • Fishing line

Construction

Note: Adult help will be needed when cutting the bottle in step 2 and using the awl in step 4.

1. Cut out your wings and tail sections.
2. Cut two openings on each side of the bottle for the wings and tail section. The two front openings need to be the same length—the width of the wings, and the two back openings need to be the same length—the width of the tail section. The wings will slide through the front openings. Two of the tail sections will slide through the back openings.
3. Cut an opening on the top of the bottle above the two back openings for the final portion of the tail.
4. Open and attach two large paper clips to the top of the airplane. One in the front and one in the rear. (If the children need help, punch the holes for their paper clips.) The paper clips will hold the airplane on the fishing line.

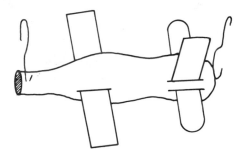

5. Stretch the fishing line from one side of the room to the other and attach it at a suitable height. (More children can participate at one time if the line is long or if you have more than one line.)
6. Attach the balloon to the rear of the bottle with masking tape.

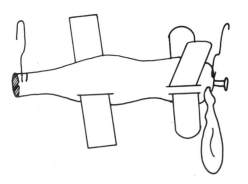

7. Position the airplane on the wire and blow up the balloon, or blow up the balloon and position the airplane on the wire. Release the balloon and watch the airplane travel along the wire.

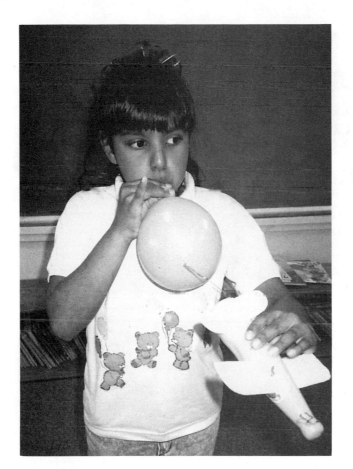

Snags and Suggestions

◆ It takes experimentation to find the best way to attach the balloon. You will need to reposition the balloon until it works.

◆ Does your airplane come off the wire? It may be too light. Try adding a pilot made of clay or a small box cockpit.

- ◆ If you become frustrated, let gravity help. Lower one end of your fishing line.
- ◆ Measure the distance each airplane travels. Make a graph of your results.

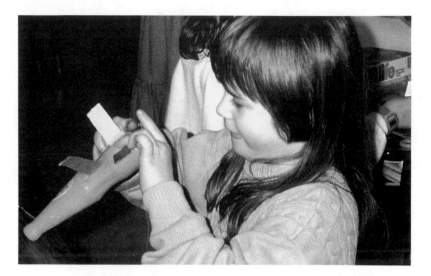

Related Literature

Hissey, Jane. *Old Bear.* New York: Putnam, 1982.
Munsch, Robert. *Angela's Airplane.* Buffalo, N.Y.: Firefly Books, 1988.

Pneumatic-Powered Boat

Materials

Plastic shampoo bottles
Straight-edged pruning shears or scissors
Power drill with 3/8-inch bit
Vinyl tubing (outside diameter of 3/8 inch)
Balloons • Masking tape • Large nails
Water table or wading pool

Construction

Note: Adult help will be needed when using the pruning shears in step 1 and when using the power drill in step 2.

1. Cut a shampoo bottle in half lengthwise. (We find that straight-edged pruning shears are wonderful cutters.)
2. Drill a hole in the bottom of the shampoo bottle. Make certain the drilled hole is as close to the cut edge as possible.
3. Cut the vinyl tubing in 8-inch lengths. Insert the tubing through the drilled hole.
4. Put the balloon over the end of the vinyl tubing that is in the boat. Use masking tape to secure it to the tubing.
5. Use masking tape to hold a nail to the bottom of the boat. The masking tape must continue up the side and into the inside of the boat so that water will not loosen the tape.
6. Blow up the balloon. Plug the end of the vinyl tubing with your thumb or finger while placing the boat in the water. Once the vinyl tubing is submerged, release your thumb or finger.

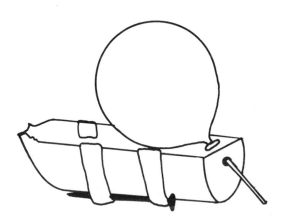

Snags and Suggestions

◆ Experiment with blowing the balloon to different sizes. How is the speed or distance affected? Make a graph.

◆ Are you having trouble with air leaking? Check the seal between the tubing and the balloon.

◆ Is your boat releasing energy too quickly and not going anywhere? Add weight to the inside of your boat. Small rocks may help. How many rocks can a boat hold and still move?

Related Literature

Fowler, Richard. *Mr. Little's Noisy Boat*. New York: Putnam, 1986.
Pfanner, Louise. *Louis Builds a Boat*. New York: Orchard Books, 1990.

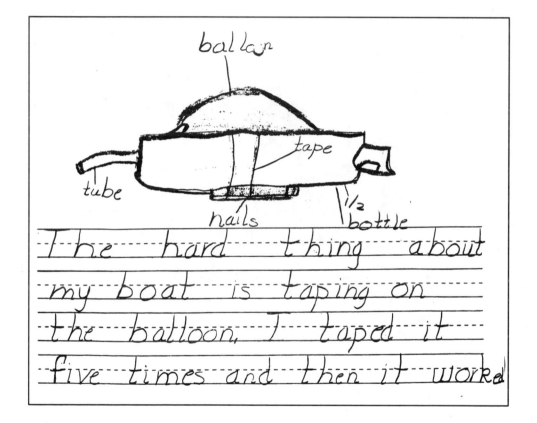

The hard thing about my boat is taping on the balloon. I taped it five times and then it worked

Dump Truck with a Pneumatic Lift

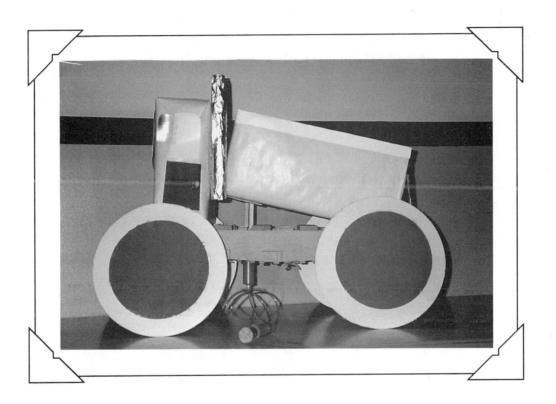

Materials

Boxes • 1-inch x 1-inch wooden strips
(length will be determined by size of box) • Cardboard
Wood glue • Pattern for axle supports (page 38)
Awl • Wheels (ribbon reels, lids, wooden wheels)
Spacers (vinyl tubing, beads, straws, cork)
Doweling • Saw
Craft supplies for decorating
Two 6-cc syringes for each truck
Vinyl tubing with 1/4-inch outside diameter

Construction

Note: Adult help will be needed when cutting the wood in step 2 and the doweling in step 6 and when using the awl in steps 5 and 11.

1. Select a box with sides as tall as the syringes, about 2 inches. The box will be part of the base of the dump truck.
2. Cut four wooden strips to make a rectangle that will be the same size as the bottom of the box. Glue the strips together.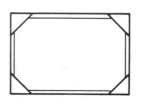
3. Cut eight cardboard triangular corners and glue them onto the top and bottom of the wooden base at each corner.
4. Glue the box to the wooden part of the base.
5. Use the pattern to cut four triangular axle supports and punch a hole in each. Strength is important. Reinforce the axle supports if necessary. Glue them onto the sides of the base toward the front and toward the back.

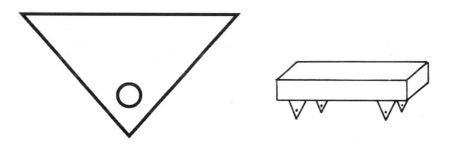

6. Make the wheel and spacer selections. Cut the doweling the width of the base plus two wheels and two spacers.
7. Insert the doweling through the axle supports. Assemble the spacers and the wheels on each side of the axle.
8. Design and construct a cab for the dump truck.
9. Select a box for the dump truck bed. To make the dump truck gate, cut the back of the box along the bottom and the sides. Score the top edge of the gate. It must swing freely.

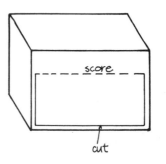

10. Decorate the sides and front of the dump truck bed.
11. Cut a hole in the middle of the bottom of the cardboard box that is the base (not the cardboard box that is the bed). The hole needs to be just large enough for the syringe. Push the syringe through the hole, leaving the tip hanging down. The syringe needs to be vertical.
12. Glue or tape the syringe plunger to the bottom of the box that is the bed of the dump truck.
13. Attach vinyl tubing to the point of the syringe under the dump truck bed and to the second syringe. Make sure the plunger of the syringe in the base is all the way down and the plunger of the second syringe is out as far as possible.
14. Push the plunger in to raise the dump truck's bed. Pull it out to have the bed of the dump truck return to its down position.
15. What different objects can you find to dump out of your truck?

Snags and Suggestions

◆ Due to the expense, this is a good project to do cooperatively either in small groups or as a total class.

◆ If you are can get two huge ribbon spools and a wooden crate, you can make a big dump truck as we did.

◆ A small dump truck can be made with 6-cc syringes. We used 60-cc syringes for a large dump truck. Vinyl tubing with a 3/8 inch outside diameter is needed for 60-cc syringes.

◆ By adding water to the syringes and tubing, you change from pneumatic power to hydraulic power. Which gives you more power, pneumatic or hydraulic?

Related Literature

Barton, Byron. *Machines at Work*. New York: Harper and Row Junior Books, 1987.

Burton, Virginia Lee. *Katy and the Big Snow*. Boston: Houghton Mifflin, 1974.

Pneumatic
Pop-Up Toy

Materials

Half-gallon milk cartons ◆ Scissors
Craft supplies for decorating
Toilet paper rolls ◆ Hot-glue gun
Large old felt-tip markers or vinyl tubing
Awl ◆ Balloons ◆ Tape ◆ Straws

Construction

Note: Adult help will be needed when using the hot-glue gun in steps 4 and 10 and the awl in step 8.

1. Select a half-gallon milk carton and cut off the top so that the carton is one inch higher than the toilet paper roll.
2. Wrap the milk carton with decorative paper.
3. Cut two platforms from the unused portion of the milk carton or from cardboard and wrap them. Make sure the platforms fit loosely inside the milk carton.
4. Wrap a toilet paper roll and glue this column to the center of one of the platforms. Set this aside.
5. On one side of the milk carton near the bottom, cut a hole the size of the large end of the felt-tip marker or the size of the vinyl tubing
6. If you are using old felt-tip pens, remove the inside and clean.
7. Insert the felt-tip marker or tubing into the milk carton and attach a balloon. Tape the balloon onto the end.
8. Measure 1 inch down from the top and 1 inch in from the edges and punch two holes on each side of the milk carton.
9. Place the platform attached to the column inside the milk carton and insert four straws through the holes to form a support for the column.
10. Glue the top platform to the top of the column.

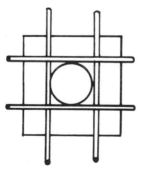

11. Test the movement of the platform by blowing through the marker or tubing, inflating the balloon.

12. Make and decorate an object that relates to your theme. Place it on the platform.

Snags and Suggestions

◆ The height of your column may need to be adjusted to the height of your milk carton.

◆ Can you figure out a way to eliminate the need for the supporting straws?

◆ If possible, decorate the outside of the box to correlate with the object on the platform.

Related Literature

Mayer, Mercer. *What Do You Do With a Kangaroo?* New York:
  Scholastic, 1987.
McNally, Darcie. *In a Cabin in a Wood.* New York:
  Cobblehill/Dutton, 1991.

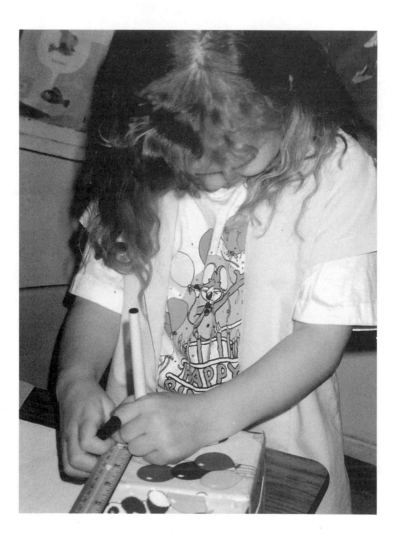

Hydraulic-Powered Plant

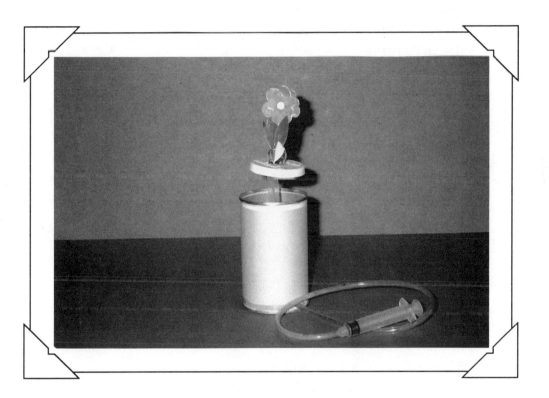

Materials

Juice containers, 12-oz. • Awl
Two syringes, 5-cc or 10-cc, for each plant
Hot-glue gun
Aquarium tubing (1/4-inch outside diameter)
Cardboard • Scissors
Craft supplies for decorating

Construction

Note: Adult help will be needed when using the awl in step 1 and the hot-glue gun in steps 2 and 5.

1. Punch a hole in the center of the bottom of a juice container. The hole needs to be large enough to allow the small end of one syringe to protrude.
2. Apply hot glue to the exterior of the small end of a syringe. Immediately insert the syringe through the bottom of the container, from the inside, making sure the small end of the syringe protrudes out of the punched hole.

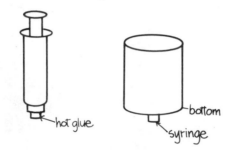

3. Attach about 18 inches of tubing to the small opening of the syringe.
4. Fill the tubing and a second syringe with water. Arrange the syringes and tubing as shown.
5. Cut a circular cardboard base to just fix inside the juice can. Glue it onto the plunger of the syringe that is in the container.

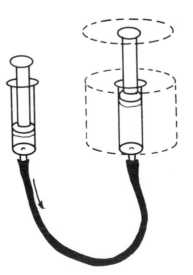

6. Design a plant or flower. Be creative!
7. Attach the plant or flower to the base inside the container.
8. Decorate the outside of the container.
9. Plunge the syringe to move the plant.

Snags and Suggestions

◆ If you would rather have your container sit flat, try running your tubing out of the side. What modifications will you need to make inside the container?

◆ If you find water is too messy, try pneumatic power. Do you notice a difference in pressure?

Related Literature

Carle, Eric. *The Tiny Seed.* Saxonville, Mass.: Picture Book Studio, 1987.

Ehlert, Lois. *Red Leaf, Green Leaf.* San Diego: Harcourt Brace Jovanovich, 1991.

Clock with Gears

Materials

Felt-tip pens • Sturdy paper plates • Awl
Pattern for clock hands and gears on page 52
Scissors • Heavy tagboard
Brads • Beads for knobs

Note: Adult help will be needed when using the awl in steps 3 and 5, and 10.

1. Using a felt-tip pen, write the clock numbers on the front of a paper plate.
2. Measure and mark the center of the plate and punch a hole.
3. Cut two hands for the clock. Place the shorter hand on top of the longer hand and punch a hole through both.
4. Insert a brad through the hole in both hands and through the center hole in the plate. Set aside.
5. Trace the patterns for the gears on heavy tagboard and cut them out. Punch holes where indicated.
6. Insert a brad through the noncentral hole in the large gear and attach the bead as a knob.
7. Bend the cogs up on the large gear.
8. Position the center of the large gear at the center of the plate and secure it with the brad.
9. Position the smaller gear to align the cogs.

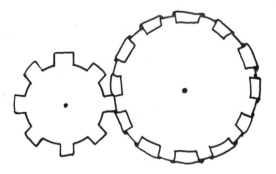

10. After aligning the gears, use the center hole of the small gear as a guide for punching a hole through the paper plate. Fasten with a brad.
11. Turn the knob.

Snags and Suggestions

◆ You will quickly discover that though the hands on your clock move, they do not move like the hands of a clock. We are not licensed clock makers.

Related Literature

Aylesworth, Jim. *The Completed Hickory Dickory Dock*. New York: Atheneum-Macmillan, 1990.

Carle, Eric. *The Grouchy Ladybug*. New York: Harper and Row Junior Books, 1986.

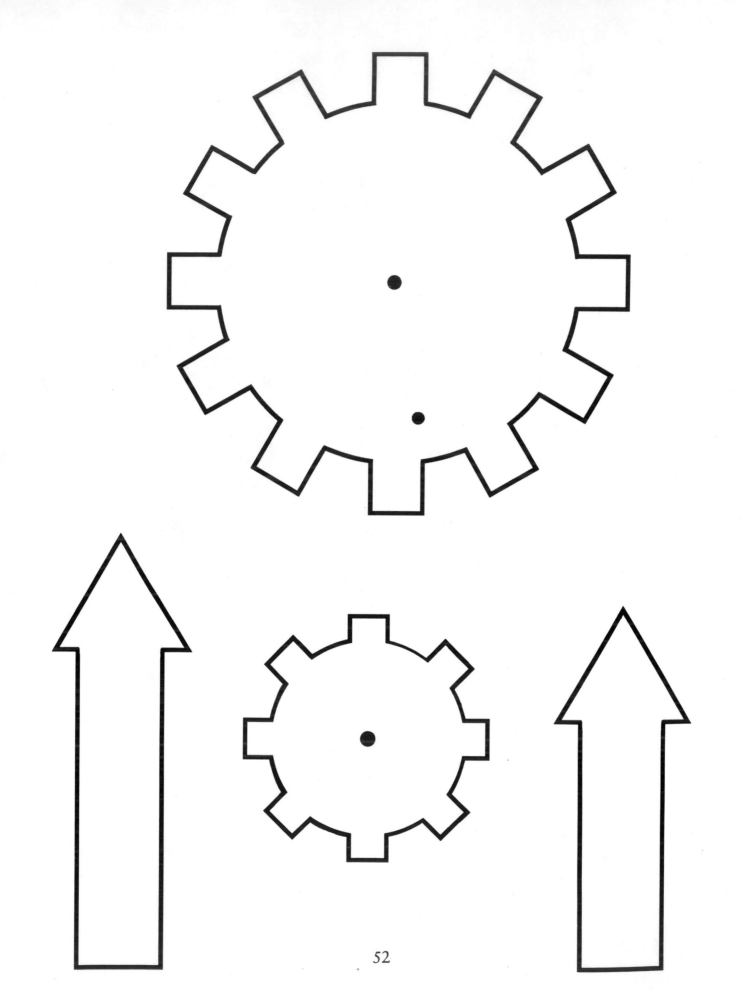

Movable Santa—A Pulling Force

Materials

Santa pattern pieces on pages 56–58
Colored tagboard • Scissors
Paper punch • Brads
Glue • String
Beads or bells for pullers
Cotton and craft supplies for decorating

Construction

1. The pattern for a Santa is given, but you can use the proportions of this pattern for other characters.
2. Trace the pattern pieces on tagboard in the appropriate colors. Remember to make two arms, two legs, and two mittens.
3. Cut the pieces out and punch holes for the brads where they are indicated.
4. Attach the head and hat and the beard to the upper body with a brad.
5. Attach the upper body to the lower body.
6. Attach the arms and boots. When attaching the arms and the boots, the brads need to go through the holes farthest from the top edge.
7. Attach the mittens with glue or a brad.
8. Cut approximately one yard of string. Thread it through the remaining four holes as in the picture.
9. Bring the string through the bead and knot. Pull the string to make the arms and boots move.
10. Decorate the Santa or other character using cotton and craft supplies of your choice.

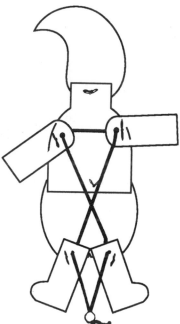

Snags and Suggestions

◆ The principles of movement are easily adapted to other themes. We have made penguins, bears, and clowns. Let your imagination soar.

Related Literature

Van Allsburg, Chris. *Polar Express*. Boston: Houghton Mifflin, 1985.

Broger, Achim. *The Santa Clauses*. New York: Dial Books for Young Readers, 1986.

56

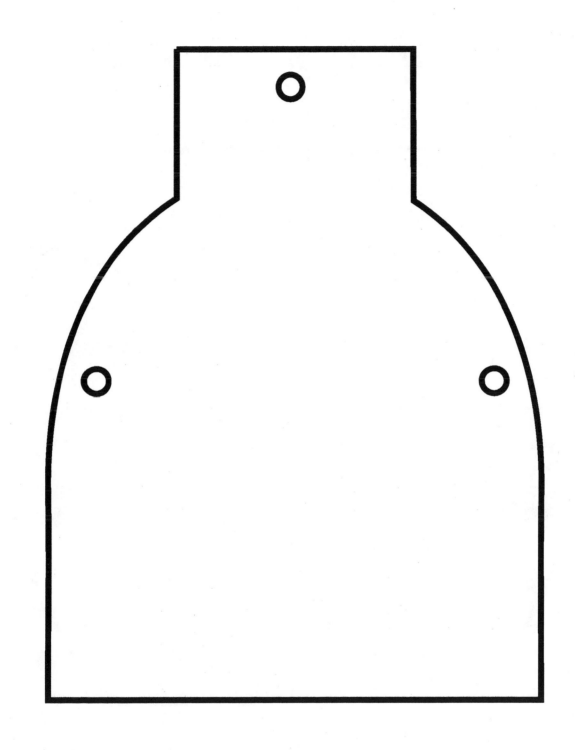

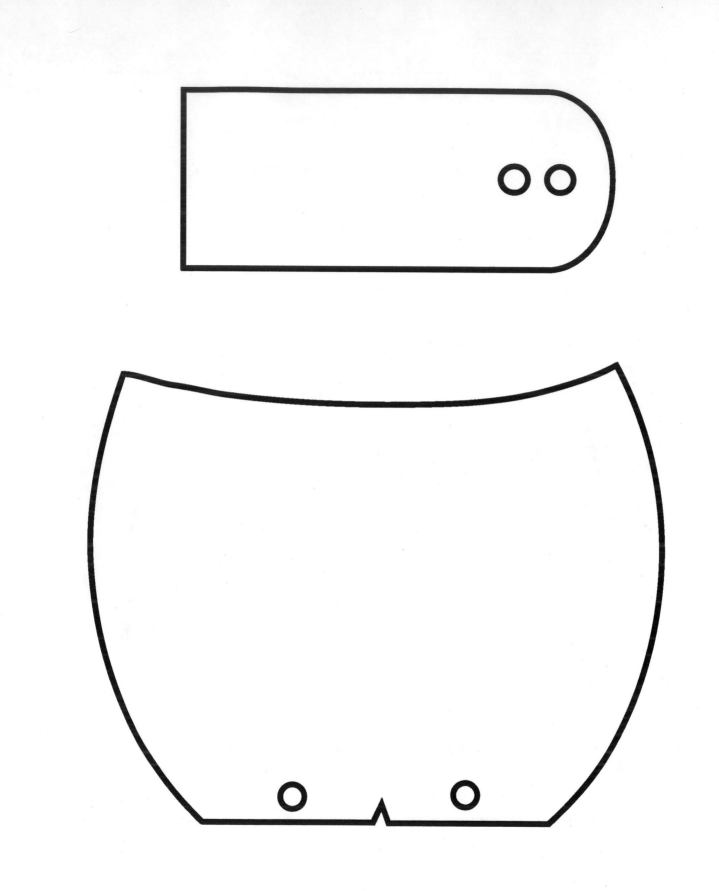

Levered Kangaroo—A Compelling Force

Materials

Kangaroo pattern pieces on pages 61–64
Tape • Brown tagboard (two shades)
Scissors • Paper punch
Awl • Brads

Construction

Note: Adult help will be needed when using the awl in step 2.

1. Tape together the two pattern pieces for the mother kangaroo. Trace the pattern pieces on tagboard in the appropriate colors, using the lighter color for the joey.
2. Cut out the pieces and punch holes for the brads where indicated. Most of the holes can be punched with the paper punch, but you will need the awl for the hole in the middle of the body.
3. To make the assembly easier, label the punched holes A, B, C, D, and E, as indicated on the pattern.
4. Assemble the kangaroo using five brads. Connect all the C holes using one brad. Do the same for the A, B, D, and E holes.
5. As the tail is moved, the joey will move up and down in the pouch!

Snags and Suggestions

◆ It is crucial to trace the patterns carefully and to punch the holes in the correct places.
◆ If two colors of brown tagboard are not available, you may color your own joey on manila tagboard.

Related Literature

Powzyk, Joyce. *Wallaby Creek.* Wooster, Ohio: Lathrop, Norman, Enterprises, 1985.

Vaughan, Marcia K. *Wombat Stew.* Morristown, N. J.: Silver Burdett and Ginn, 1986.

B

E O

A O

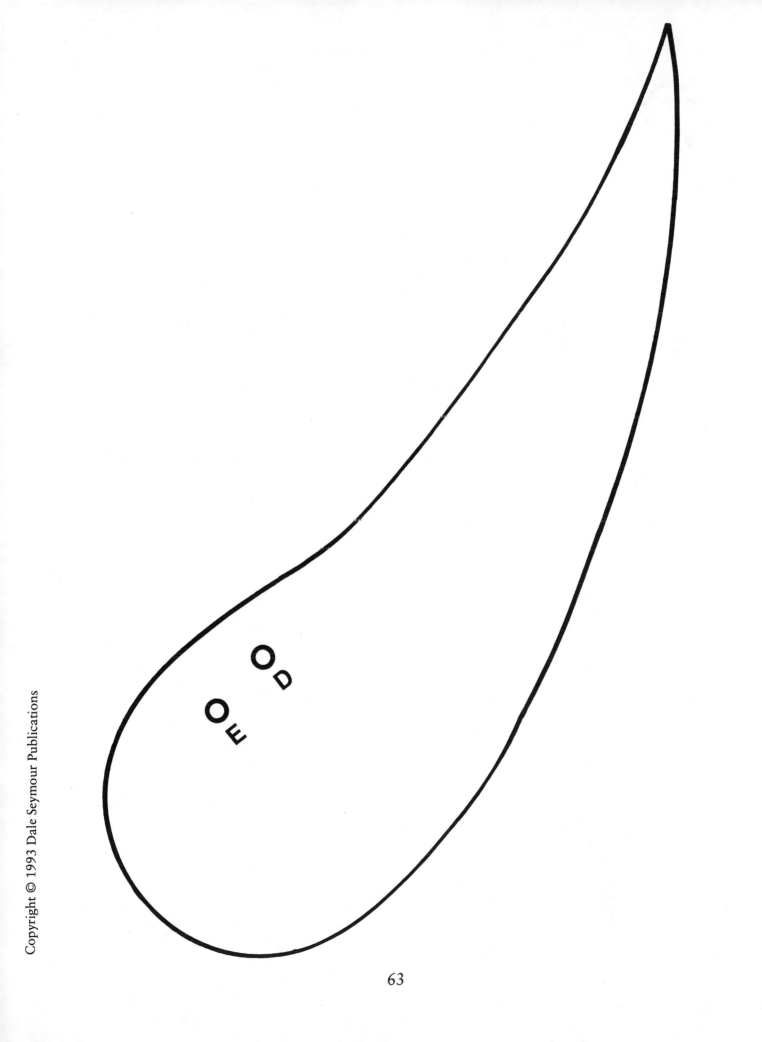

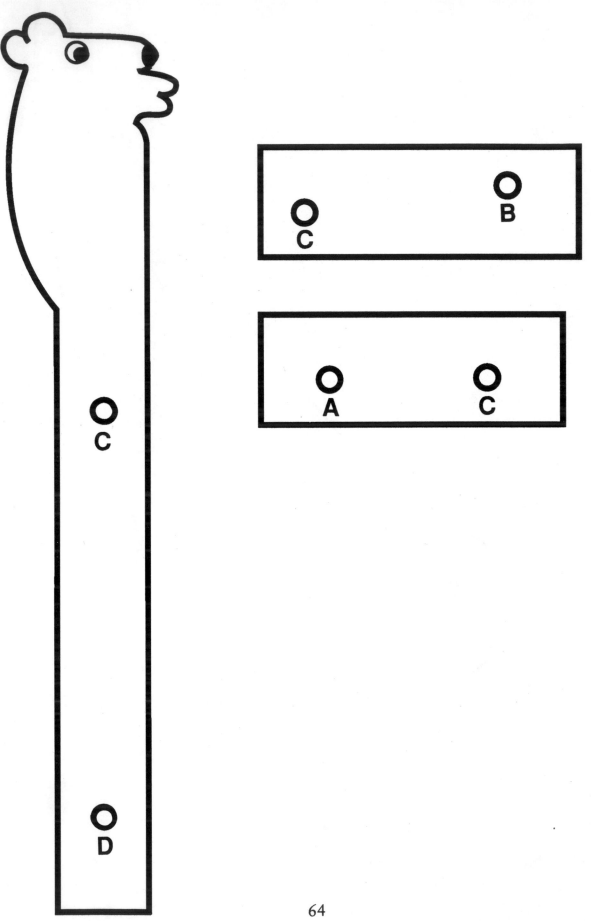

Hopping Kangaroo
with a Drive Mechanism

Materials

Wire • Wire cutters • Pliers
Paper clips • Masking tape
Containers (butter tubs, topping containers)
Awl • Heavyweight paper
Decorating materials

Construction

Note: Adult help is needed when using wire cutters and pliers in step 1 and the awl in step 4.

1. Cut a piece of wire for the crank, and bend it into a crank in the shape shown. The size of the container will determine the width and the height of the center section of the drive mechanism and the finished length of the crank.

2. Open a paper clip and attach it to the center of the drive mechanism.

3. Apply masking tape to each side of the paper clip to keep it stationary.

4. Punch a hole in the center of the bottom of the container. Punch two holes opposite each other in the sides of the containers (approximately halfway up).

5. Working from the center, insert the wires through the holes. Put the paper clip through the hole in the bottom of the container. It will help to keep the crank stationary.

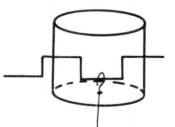

6. Apply masking tape where indicated in the sketch.

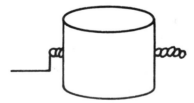

7. On heavy paper draw the front and the back of a kangaroo or other character. Make the two pieces the same size and shape, but color and decorate them differently.

8. Attach the front of the kangaroo and the back of the kangaroo to the paper clip and the center section of the crank.

9. We hope you will enjoy turning the crank as much as we do!

Snags and Suggestions

◆ We found #14 galvanized anchor wire works very well for the crank.

◆ This drive-mechanism project can be adapted to many different themes by changing the animal.

◆ This project can show a practical example of using fractions. You can stretch two rubber bands over the container and divide the container into fourths as evenly as possible. This will help you find the correct place for all the necessary holes.

Related Literature

Trinca, Rod, and Kerry Argent. *One Woolly Wombat*. New York: Kane-Miller Books, 1985.

Kent, Jack. *Joey Runs Away*. New York: Simon and Schuster, 1991.

Marionette Ant

Materials

Wheat paste ◆ Paper cups ◆ Newspaper
Masking tape ◆ Small paper clips
Pipe cleaners ◆ Tempera paint
Hot-glue gun ◆ Chopsticks ◆ String

Construction

Note: Adult help is needed when using the hot-glue gun in step 8.

1. Mix with water approximately one-third of a 5-pound bag of wheat paste and divide it into paper cups or other disposable containers. This will make plenty of paste for the whole class.
2. Crumple newspaper into three balls for the three sections of the ant's body. Tape each ball to hold its shape.
3. Open one end of each of four paper clips and tape them into position on the bottom of each section. These will be used to attach the body sections together.

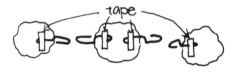

4. Cut two pipe cleaners in half. Tape three of the four pieces onto the bottom of the center section of the ant to form the six legs.

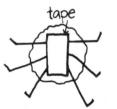

5. Cut the fourth piece of pipe cleaner in half and bend each piece into an "L" shape. Tape the pieces of pipe cleaner onto the top of the head section to form the antennae.
6. Tear strips of newspaper and dip them into the paste. Wrap them around the balls, leaving the hooks, legs, and antennae exposed. Let the ant sections dry for several days.
7. Paint each section with tempera paint.
8. Bend the large part of three small paper clips sideways to a 90° angle and, using a hot-glue gun, attach them to the tops of each section.
9. Hook the three ant sections together.

10. Cut three pieces of string, each 7 to 8 inches long, and tie one to each of the 90°-angled paper clips. Tape the other ends of the strings to two chopsticks, taping the string that is attached to the head to one chopstick and the remaining two strings to the other chopstick.

11. Bend the middle-section pipe cleaners to look like legs.

12. Decorate the face of the ant.

13. Move the chopsticks to simulate the ant walking.

Snags and Suggestions

◆ To simplify, you may wish to cut the strings and have the paper clips bent before you start.

◆ The ants can be used to inspire conversational writing and plays.

Related Literature

Dorros, Arthur. *Ant Cities*. New York: Harper and Row Junior
    Books, 1988.
Van Allsburg, Chris. *Two Bad Ants*. Boston: Houghton Mifflin,
    1988.

Marionette Crocodile

Pattern for crocodile on page 76 ✦ Plastic foam sheets
Colored tagboard ✦ Glue ✦ Awl
Yarn ✦ Small lids ✦ String
Wooden sticks (tongue depressors, ice cream sticks)
Hot-glue gun ✦ Masking tape

Construction

Note: Adult help will be needed when using the awl in steps 4, 5, and 7 and when using the hot-glue gun in step 6.

1. Trace the pattern pieces of the crocodile on a sheet of plastic foam and cut them out.
2. Trace each pattern piece twice on colored tagboard and cut out.
3. Glue the plastic foam pieces between the colored tagboard pieces. Put weight on the pieces to eliminate curling while the glue dries.
4. Using an awl, punch two holes in the body of the crocodile for the legs and thread the yarn through the holes.
5. Using the awl, punch a hole in the center of four small lids. Thread the yarn through the lids and knot it on the bottom.
6. Select three wooden sticks and glue them together as shown.

7. Punch a hole in the top of the head and the top of the body. Thread a string through each hole and tie.
8. Tape the loose ends of the strings to the center wooden stick.
9. Tie four strings to the yarn above the feet and tape the loose ends to the other wooden sticks.
10. Decorate the crocodile's face.
11. Take your crocodile for a walk. Its feet are so special.

Snags and Suggestions

- If you would rather not punch holes in the lids for the feet, attach the yarn to the lids with tape or hot-glue.
- You may find a needle helpful for threading.
- You may want to decorate the face before you assemble the crocodile.
- We have found that hanging the crocodiles while not in use is better than laying them down.
- Let your imagination soar and create other animals. We have made elephants and ants. How about spiders?
- Use the crocodiles to inspire conversational writing and plays.

Related Literature

Dahl, Roald. *The Enormous Crocodile*. New York: Alfred A. Knopf, 1978.

Mayer, Mercer. *There's an Alligator Under My Bed*. New York: Dial Books for Young Readers, 1987.

76

Marionette Robot

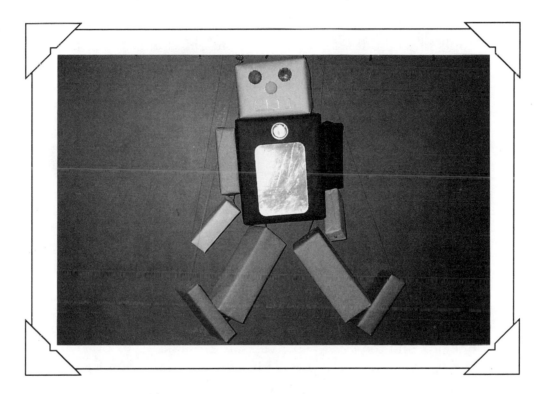

Materials

Boxes of all kinds and sizes
Butcher paper to wrap the boxes
Small paper clips • Rubber bands
Awl • Masking tape • String
Craft supplies for decorating
Tape • Doweling or bamboo

Construction

Note: Adult help will be needed when using the awl in steps 4, 5, and 10.

1. Make connectors out of two paper clips and a rubber band. Hook a paper clip to each end of a rubber band that has been doubled, and put masking tape around the ends of the paper clips to keep the rubber band near the middle. Make a minimum of ten connectors for your robot.

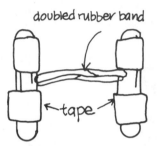

doubled rubber band

tape

2. Select at least nine boxes and wrap them with butcher paper.
3. Lay out the boxes for your robot.
4. To make the joints, punch holes in the boxes for the connectors. Insert one paper clip of a connector into the hole in one box and the other paper clip into the hole of the other box.
5. Use two connectors to join the head to the body. Punch two holes in the bottom of the head and two aligning holes in the top of the body. Insert one half of a connector into the head hole and one half of a connector into the body hole, repeat for the second hole.
6. Use one connector for each of the other joints.
7. Have fun decorating your robot.
8. Cut six lengths of string long enough to go from the feet of the robot to approximately 8 inches above the robot's head.
9. Tie the six strings to six paper clips. Put masking tape around the ends of the paper clips to keep the string near the middle.
10. Punch one hole in the top of each shoulder, one hole in the lower part of each arm, and one hole at the top of each foot. The holes are to hold the marionette strings.

11. Insert one of the six paper clips with the string attached into each hole.

12. Use two pieces of doweling or bamboo that are about 12 inches long. Tie the shoulder strings to one piece of doweling. Roll the doweling until both strings are even in length and secure with masking tape.

13. Tie the arm strings and feet strings to the other piece of doweling. Again, roll the doweling until all strings are even in length and secure with masking tape.

14. Use the two pieces of doweling to take the robot for a walk.

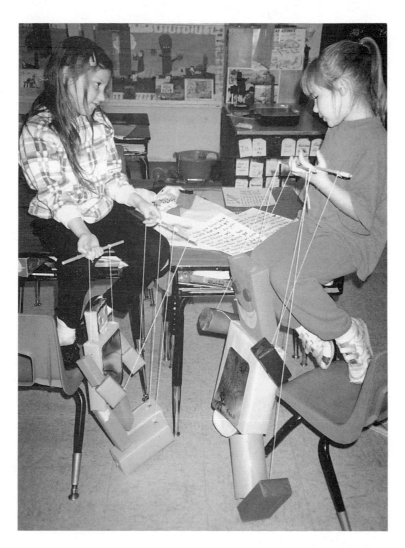

Snags and Suggestions

◆ We like to make up the connectors the day before.

◆ If you have a problem with the head falling, attach a marionette string to the center of the head or add additional connectors.

◆ We have found that unless you enjoy untangling strings, it is better to hang your robot when not in use than to lay it down.

◆ Practice your best robot voice.

◆ The robots are wonderful for developing conversational writing.

◆ Create a way to figure a cost for each robot by assigning different costs to the different-sized boxes. Find and display the total cost for each of the robots. The range of prices can be discussed and graphed.

Related Literature

Cole, Babette. *The Trouble With Dad*. New York: Putnam, 1986.

Dupasquier, Phillippe. *Robot Named Chip*. New York: Viking Penguin, 1991.

Bridge

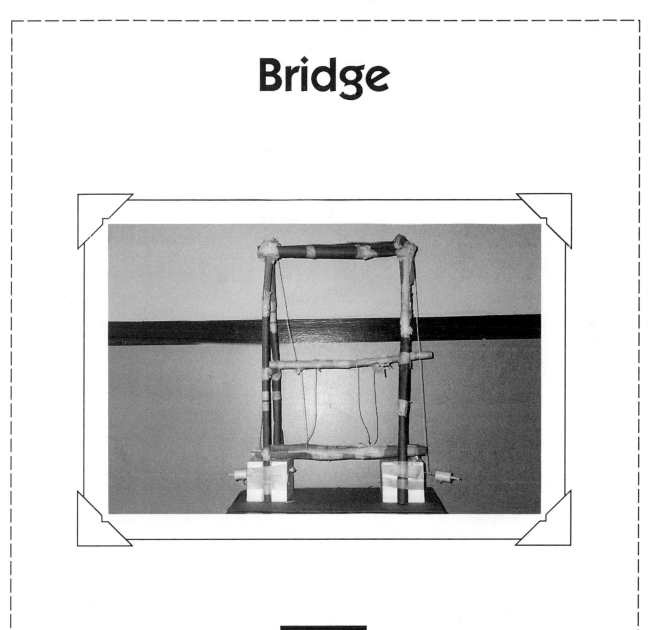

Materials

Cardboard, 12 inches × 30 inches
Boxes
Construction paper, 9 inches × 12 inches
Wood pieces, 1/2 inch × 1/2 inch × 12 inches
Glue ◆ Masking tape ◆ Scissors
String ◆ Spools ◆ Doweling ◆ Awl

Construction

Note: Adult help is needed when using the awl in step 8.

1. Using the cardboard for a base, glue boxes of the same height to each end. These form the bridge piers.

2. Select approximately ten pieces of construction paper. Take the 12-inch wood piece and lay it at the edge of a sheet of construction paper. Roll the paper, creasing it at the corners of the wood piece. Continue this pattern of rolling and creasing until the paper is completely rolled up. Apply a thin line of glue to the final edge and press. Secure both ends with masking tape; then remove the wood.

3. To make a joint for additional length, pleat or tuck one end of a rolled paper length and insert it approximately 2 inches into another length. Secure the joint with masking tape.

4. To make an L-shaped joint, take one rolled paper length and cut one side on the creases, cutting down approximately 1/2 inch. Bend the cut section down and set another length into it. Secure with masking tape.

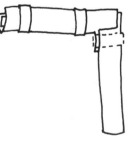

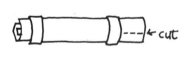

5. Depending on the type of bridge, you may need to increase the number of supports. A suspension bridge would take fewer supports than a drawbridge.

6. Each bridge needs to have enough supports to hold a roadway. You can make a roadway by using masking tape to join rolled paper lengths together.

7. If you choose to make a drawbridge, you will need to select a length of string long enough to go from the roadway up over the supports and down to the piers. Secure the string to the roadway and attach it to a spool with masking tape.

8. To complete the drawbridge, poke a hole in the pier for a piece of doweling. Place the spool on the doweling. Wrap masking tape around the doweling until it is thick enough to keep the spool from coming off. Slide the spool down the dowel to lift the bridge.

9. If you choose to make a suspension bridge, use string for the cables that support the roadway.

10. If you choose to make a swing-span bridge, make a center pier and attach the roadway with a brad. Secure with masking tape.

Snags and Suggestions

◆ For a sturdy bridge, it is very important to roll the supports carefully.

◆ If the bridge is leaning, check the joints.

◆ Your bridge must accommodate a vehicle. Choose your vehicle before you build your bridge.

◆ This is an excellent partner project.

◆ We built a web to organize all the information the children had learned about bridges. You could also start a web on bridges at the beginning of your project, and add to it as students find out more information.

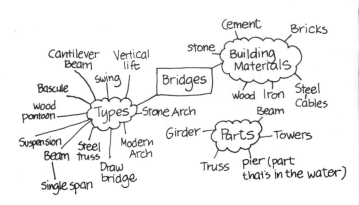

Related Literature

Baker, Keith. *Magic Fan*. San Diego, Calif.: Harcourt Brace Jovanovich, 1989.

Spier, Peter. *London Bridge Is Falling Down*. New York: Doubleday, 1985.

Professional Resources

Aitken, John and George Mills. *Scientific Problem Solving: An Introduction to Technology*. Belmont, Calif.: David S. Lake, 1989.

Andrew, Meira. *Language In Colour*. Twickenham, England: Belair, 1989.

Booth, W., P. Briten and F. Scott. *Themes Familiar*. Twickenham, England: Belair, 1987.

Child Education. Warwickshire, England: Scholastic, 1989.

Dunn, Susan and Rob Larson. *Design Technology: Children's Engineering*. Bristal, Pa.: The Falmer Press, 1990.

Hume, Barbara and Kathie Barrs. *Maths on Display*. Twickenham, England: Belair, 1988.

Junior Projects. Warwickshire, England: Scholastic, 1989.

Macaulay, David. *The Way Things Work*. Boston: Houghton Mifflin, 1988.

Makreff, Judith and Linda Duncan. *Display for All Seasons*. Twickenham, England: Belair, 1989.

McCormick, Alan J. *Inventor's Workshop*. Belmont, Calif.: David S. Lake, 1981.

Radford, Don. *Science from Toys*. London: MacDonald Education, 1973.

Radford, Don. *Science, Models and Toys*. London: MacDonald Education, 1974.

Williams, Pat, and David Jinks. *Design and Technology*. Bristol Pa.: The Falmer Press, 1985.

The Belair publications can be ordered from:
    Heffers Booksellers
    20 Trinity Street
    Cambridge, England CB23NG

The Scholastic publications can be ordered from:
    Scholastic Publications Ltd.
    Westfield Road
    Southam
    Leamington Spa
    Warwickshire, England CV330BR

The MacDonald Education publications can be ordered from:
    Teachers Laboratory
    P.O. Box 6480
    Brattleboro, VT 05302-6480
    802 254-3457